This igloo book belongs to:

....

igloobooks

Published in 2016
by Igloo Books Ltd
Cottage Farm
Sywell
NN6 0BJ
www.igloobooks.com

Copyright © 2007 Igloo Books Ltd

HUN001 0816
4 6 8 10 9 7 5 3
ISBN 978-1-78557-090-2

Printed and manufactured in China

My First Bible Stories

Retold by Nick Ellsworth

Illustrated by
Roger Langton and
Sara Sliwinska

igloobooks

The Old Testament

THE NEW TESTAMENT

THE OLD TESTAMENT

In The Beginning

GENESIS 1-2

In the beginning there was God. Then God created Earth. But to begin with, Earth was as dark as night. So God said, "Let there be light!" So He made the Sun. Now there was day to go with night.

Then God made the sky and, underneath the sky, He gathered together huge amounts of water to make the seas.

And in between the seas He made rocks and mountains and soil. Then He made flowers and forests of trees which could grow in the soil.

Then God made fish that could live in the seas and birds that could fly in the sky and animals that could live on the land.

He then made the first man, whom He called Adam. God thought Adam might be lonely all by himself, so He made the first woman, whom He called Eve.

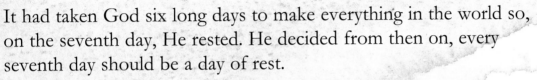

It had taken God six long days to make everything in the world so, on the seventh day, He rested. He decided from then on, every seventh day should be a day of rest.

And this special day of rest He called the Sabbath.

Adam and Eve

GENESIS 2-3

God gave Adam and Eve a beautiful garden to live in, which He called the Garden of Eden. He filled it with the loveliest flowers and plants. There were rivers Adam and Eve could drink from, and trees bearing the most delicious fruit. It was truly paradise.

In the center of the garden, God planted a special tree.
"This is the Tree of Knowledge of Good and Evil," He told them.
"Do not eat the fruit that grows on it. If you do, you will die."

Adam and Eve lived happily in the garden for many years and made sure that they never ate the fruit that grew on the special tree.

But, one day, a slimy snake slithered up to Eve and hissed, "You really should taste the apples that grow on the Tree of Knowledge. They really are the most delicious fruit in the garden."

Eve was a little frightened.

"But God said we'd die if we tasted the fruit from that tree," she said.

"You won't die!" mocked the snake. "God said that because He knows if you were to eat the fruit, you would become as wise as He, and He wouldn't want that to happen, would He?"

Eve thought this made sense. So she walked slowly to the Tree of Knowledge, picked off the juiciest, ripest apple she could see, and took a big bite out of it. And, when she saw Adam a little later, she shared the fruit with him.

When God realized what they had done, He was angry.
"You have disobeyed me," He said. "You must now leave this beautiful garden. From this day on, you must work hard to grow your own food in the rough and thorny ground that lies beyond here. And when you grow old, you will die."

So Adam and Eve left the Garden of Eden. Their lives became much harder, and they struggled to grow enough to eat in the hot, harsh lands outside the Garden of Eden.

For the rest of their days, they regretted the time when they disobeyed God by eating the fruit that grew on the Tree of Knowledge.

Cain and Abel

GENESIS 4

Adam and Eve had two sons. One was named Cain, the other, Abel. Cain worked in the fields growing crops while his brother Abel looked after the sheep on the hills.

They both grew up loving God and tried to please Him in any way they could.

Once, Cain offered some of his freshly cut crops to God, while Abel offered Him one of his newborn lambs. God was pleased with Abel's lamb but did not want Cain's crops, thinking they were not worthy of Him.

Cain was jealous that God had accepted Abel's offering, but not his own. One day he suggested to his brother that they should go for a walk together. While they were out, Cain killed his brother.

When Cain returned home, God asked him where Abel was.
"I don't know," replied Cain. "Am I my brother's keeper?"
But God knew what he had done and said, "Your brother's blood
cries out to me from the ground. You will be punished for your evil.
You will spend the rest of your life wandering the Earth, and you will
find no rest."
"But I will be killed by the first person who sees me," cried Cain.
"You will not," said God. "I will put a mark on you that tells
people that if they dare to kill you, I will take seven lives in revenge."

So Cain collected his few belongings and left his home forever.

Noah's Ark

GENESIS 6-9

God was angry. He saw that most people on Earth were not obeying him, so He decided to flood the whole world and drown everyone in it.

But there was one man He decided to save. This man's name was Noah. God knew that Noah was a good man and wanted to save him from the flood.

"You and your family must build a great Ark," God told him. "In it, you will gather together two of every animal on Earth. Do this and you will be saved."

Noah and his family set to work. They cut down the tallest trees and used them to make the frame of the Ark. Then they covered the frame with rough planks of wood and put tar on the inside so that water couldn't get in.

They all worked very hard for many months. Finally, it was finished.

25

Noah then gathered together two of every single creature on Earth, just as God had told him to do. The animals lined up and slowly began to file into the Ark. There were so many of them, it took a very long time. Everyone helped to load enough food and water to last them for months. Once Noah and his family had joined the animals on board, Noah shut the huge doors behind them.

Then, the rains began.

It rained for forty days and forty nights. Soon, the whole Earth was covered with water and became one big sea.

For months and months, the Ark tossed around on the sea. Noah peered through the windows every day, hoping to see signs of dry land, but he saw only water.

One day he sent out a raven to look for dry land, but the raven didn't return.

Then he sent out a dove to look for dry land, but the dove didn't return, either.

Noah sent out a second dove. When it returned with an olive branch in its beak, Noah knew this was a sign that the waters were going down, and dry land wasn't too far away.

He sent out the dove once more and this time it didn't return. Noah now knew beyond doubt that the flood had almost disappeared. He looked out of a window and was overjoyed to see dry land on the horizon.

Gathering his family together, Noah told them the news they had waited so long to hear. Then they sailed happily towards the shore.

After he had made sure all the animals
left the Ark safely, Noah got down
on one knee and thanked God for
keeping his family safe.

"I promise," said God, "however angry I become, I will never again destroy what I have created."

Then He put a beautiful rainbow in the sky.
"Whenever I see a rainbow," said God, "it will remind me to keep my promise. And when you see a rainbow, think of my promise and be certain that I will keep it."

29

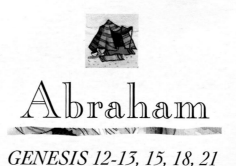

Abraham

GENESIS 12-13, 15, 18, 21

Abraham was one of Noah's descendants. He was a wealthy man and lived with his wife, Sarah, in a place called Haran. Although Abraham and Sarah had a happy life together, their one great sadness was that they had no children.

One day, God spoke to Abraham.
"I want you to take everything you own and go and live in the land of Canaan. There, I will make you the father of a great nation."
Abraham loved God, so he did as God asked. He gathered together all his sheep and goats, and made the long journey to Canaan with Sarah. His nephew Lot, and Lot's wife, also went with them.

At first, there was plenty of grass and water for Abraham's animals but, as the years passed and his flock grew bigger, there wasn't enough to feed them all.
"Let me go and live further down the valley," said Lot. "There will be much more grass and water down there."
Abraham would miss Lot, but knew it was the right thing to do.

Some years later, Abraham saw three men passing by close to his tent. He invited them in to share a meal with him. When they had finished eating, one of the men told Abraham that he had a message for him, from God.

"You and Sarah are going to have a baby," the man smiled.

"But Sarah is far too old to have a baby!" Abraham exclaimed.

To his amazement, some months later Sarah gave birth to a baby boy. They named him Isaac. It was then that Abraham remembered God's words from many years ago: "I will make you the father of a great nation."

Abraham was very proud that his son Isaac would be the first child of that nation.

Moses in the Bulrushes

EXODUS 1-2

Many years after Joseph, Isaac's grandson, died, a new King came to power in Egypt. He hated the Hebrews and made them work as slaves, doing all the dirtiest and hardest jobs that the Egyptians didn't want to do. The King made them work very long hours and they were whipped and beaten if they tried to rest.

As there were more and more Hebrews being born in Egypt every year, the King became afraid that they would one day turn against their Egyptian masters and take over the whole country. So he ordered his soldiers to kill every Hebrew boy as soon as he was born. One clever Hebrew mother managed to hide her baby until he was three months old. After that, he was getting too big to hide, so she had to think of another way to protect him. His mother had named him Moses.

She took him down to the water's edge of the great Nile River and set him afloat in a small basket made of reeds. She was sad to see him float away, but knew it was the only way to save him. Her daughter, Miriam, followed the little basket as it floated away.

Some distance down the river, an Egyptian Princess was bathing in its clear waters. She noticed the basket as it bobbed its way towards her. When she looked inside, she was surprised to see a small baby.

"This must be a poor Hebrew child," she said to one of her handmaidens. The Princess felt so sorry for the little baby she decided to keep him.

Miriam, who had been hiding in the bulrushes, had an idea. She boldly approached the Princess.
"Your Highness," she said. "I know of a very caring Hebrew woman who could nurse this baby for you."

45

Moses in the Desert

EXODUS 15-17

After many weeks of walking through the barren desert, the Hebrews were tired and hungry.
"We were better off in Egypt," they said. "At least we had food and water there."

Moses was very worried but God spoke to him and comforted him. "Tell the people I will give them meat every evening and bread every morning, except on the seventh day, which will be My day of rest. That day will be called the Sabbath."

That evening, a huge flock of birds surrounded the tents where they slept. There were so many birds, they were easy to catch. At supper, the Hebrews filled their empty stomachs with the meat of the birds.

The next morning, the people looked out of their tents and saw that the ground was covered in seeds. The people gathered up as much of the seed as they could, ground it into flour, and made it into bread.

"God has sent you this bread," Moses explained. "It is called Manna."

But soon the people were complaining again.
"We have no water to drink!" they grumbled. "How can we live without water?"
Moses turned to God for help, saying to him, "These people are dying of thirst and I have no water for them."
"Take your staff and strike the first rock you see," commanded God.
Moses followed God's command. He walked up to the first rock he saw and struck it with his staff. As soon as he did so, an enormous fountain of fresh water gushed out. Now that they had water as well as food, the people were happy at last.

Orpah agreed, but brave Ruth decided to take care of Naomi and to follow her wherever she went.

When they reached Bethlehem the harvest was beginning. Having little food, Ruth went into the fields every day hoping to pick up the ears of corn that had been missed. The farmer who owned the fields was a man named Boaz. He had heard how good Ruth had been to Naomi, and offered her all the water and corn she needed.

When Ruth told Naomi of Boaz's kindness, Naomi said, "This shows that God still cares for us. Even though our loved ones are dead, He has sent Boaz to help us."

Boaz started to care for Ruth, and asked her to marry him. Ruth happily agreed. Soon after, she gave birth to a baby boy. Naomi loved the boy very much and thanked God for giving her such a beautiful grandson.

David and Goliath

1 SAMUEL 16-17

Ruth's great grandson, David, worked on his father's farm. His job was to look after the sheep that grazed on the hills. He was a fearless boy who often had to defend his sheep against wild animals such as wolves and bears. He became an expert with a slingshot, which he fired stones with, to drive the wild animals away.

For years, King Saul of the Israelites had been fighting the Philistines. Down in the valley below David, a huge battle was about to take place. On one side of the valley lay the Israelite soldiers and, on the other, the mighty Philistine army.

One day, David's father asked him to take some food to his brothers who were soldiers in the Israelite army. As David got nearer, he could see the two great armies lined up opposite each other.

Suddenly, a giant of a man stepped out from the line of Philistine soldiers.

"My name is Goliath," he shouted to the Israelites. "I am the fiercest fighter in the world! No one can beat me! I challenge one of you to fight me! If you win, you win the battle for your whole army!"

The Israelite soldiers shrank back in fear. None of them dared to fight Goliath alone. Then David stepped forward.

"I'll fight you," he said. "I'm not afraid of you."

Goliath threw his head back and roared with laughter.

"Don't be silly, little boy. I will kill you in an instant."

"No, you won't," replied David. "I have God on my side."

King Saul tried to persuade David not to fight, but David's reply was simple and brave, "Do not worry, my King. God will help me."

Saul gave David his armor, but it was far too heavy for him to wear.

57

"I just need my slingshot and my faith in God," said David.
Then the giant and the boy walked out to fight each other. David bent
down and picked up five smooth stones from the river bed.
All of a sudden, Goliath charged at him with a huge roar. David carefully
loaded his slingshot with one of the stones, took aim, and fired it at
the giant. The stone hit Goliath right between the eyes, and buried deep
in his forehead. He was stopped in an instant and fell dead at David's feet.

The Philistines could not believe that their hero, Goliath, was dead. The Israelites cheered their new hero, David, and chased the Philistine soldiers all the way back to their city gates. David was his country's savior. He became famous throughout the land and eventually, when he grew up, became King of Israel.

King David

2 SAMUEL 5-11

Many years later, when David did become King of Israel, he had many other battles to fight; he fought against people who still supported the old King, Saul, and against the Philistines who longed to return to Israel.

David had always wanted to capture Jerusalem. In time, he succeeded, and made it God's city.

David was a much-loved King, but he had weaknesses that made God sad. Once, he fell in love with a woman named Bathsheba, but she was already married to a soldier in David's army. David wanted Bathsheba so much he arranged to have her husband killed.

Afterwards, he felt so guilty he spent many days praying for God's forgiveness.

One day, two women came to see King Solomon. They had a baby with them, and each woman said that the baby belonged to her. They wanted Solomon to decide who was the real mother. "Bring me a sword," said Solomon. "I will cut the baby in half. In this way, you can share this child."

One of the women agreed to this at once, but the other cried out, "No! I would rather see my baby brought up by another woman than see my child killed."

Elijah built his altar and placed a dead bull on it.
He then soaked the animal in water and stood back and prayed to
God to send fire. Even though the bull was soaking, it burst into
flames.

"Elijah's God is the true God!" everyone cried.

Then Elijah prayed for rain. For the first time in years, the sky
grew dark and rain began to fall in Israel.
When King Ahab and his wife, Jezebel, heard what Elijah had
done, they vowed to have him killed.
Elijah fled for his life and, after a long and tiring journey, found
himself at the foot of Mount Sinai.

"I am so lonely, Lord," he said to God. "I am your only prophet
left in Israel. All the others have been killed. Now the King and
Jezebel want to kill me, too."
"I know it is dangerous and you are frightened. But you must
return," said God. "There is much work to do there."

The King Will Come

MICAH 5

There were many times that God's people disobeyed Him. Sometimes they lost their faith that He was the only true God, and were tempted to worship other gods. But the prophets knew God only wanted peace for His people and that He had great plans for their future.

They knew that one day, a new King of Israel would be born in the little town of Bethlehem. He would be God's own son and he would spread God's laws throughout the whole world.

This new King would be named Jesus, and his story is told in the New Testament.

It was nightfall by the time they arrived, tired and hungry. Even worse, all the inns where they could have stayed were full. After searching for several hours, the only place where they could find shelter was an empty stable.

Joseph made the stable as comfortable as he could for his wife, who laid down to rest. Some time later, Mary gave birth to a little baby boy. She gave thanks for his safe delivery and named him Jesus, as the angel Gabriel had asked her to.

The fishermen did as Jesus asked. When they hauled in their net, they were amazed to see it was so full of fish it was almost bursting! They called to their friends, James and John, who were fishing nearby, to help them take all the fish back to shore.

The fishermen were pleased with their catch but were frightened of Jesus's powers.
 "Do not be scared," said Jesus, gently. "Come with me and I will make you fishers of men."

Andrew, Peter, James, and John left their boats that day and followed Jesus wherever he went. They became his first disciples.

As Jesus journeyed through the country, preaching the word of God, he collected more disciples along the way. Soon there were twelve of them. Apart from the four fishermen of Galilee, there was Philip, Matthew, Thomas, Bartholomew, another James, Judas, Simon, and Judas Iscariot. They all loved Jesus, and they, too, became messengers of God.

Jesus Heals the Sick

MATTHEW 8, LUKE 7, 18

As Jesus's fame grew and grew, more people flocked to his side, hoping to catch a glimpse of him. The sick and diseased fought their way through the crowds, hoping that Jesus would heal them.

One day a blind beggar, unable to push his way to Jesus's side, shouted out, "Son of David, have mercy on me!"
Jesus heard the blind man's call and asked that he be brought to him.
"What do you want from me?" Jesus asked.
"Lord, let me see!" pleaded the beggar.
Jesus laid his hands on the man's head, and said, "Receive your sight. Your faith has healed you."
When Jesus took his hands away, the beggar could see again.

Another time, Jesus was asked to visit the house of a Roman soldier. The soldier's servant was very sick and close to death. As Jesus neared his house, the soldier rushed out to meet him.

When a woman touched Jesus's robe as he passed by, Jesus turned and asked, "Who touched me?" The woman stepped forward.

"I did, Master. I have been sick for many years. Now that I have touched your robe, I am healed."

"Your faith has made you well," said Jesus. "Go in peace."

A messenger from Jairus's house was sent out to meet them.
"I have bad news for you, Jairus," he said. "Your daughter has died."
Jairus fell to the ground with grief.

Then the soldiers led Jesus out of the garden. The disciples were so frightened, they ran away.

Later that night, Peter was asked three times if he was a friend of Jesus. Peter denied knowing him each time he was asked. When he realized what he had said, he leaned against a tree and wept.

143

Jesus on Trial

MATTHEW 27, MARK 15, LUKE 23, JOHN 18-19

The priests of the Temple had decided that Jesus must die, but they were not allowed to put anyone to death. So they had Jesus dragged in front of the Roman governor, Pontius Pilate.
He was a powerful man who had the authority to order an execution.

"What has he done wrong?" Pontius Pilate asked the priests.
"He says he is a king," they replied.
"Are you the King of the Jews?" Pontius Pilate asked Jesus.
"You say I am," said Jesus and, bowing his head, refused to answer any more questions.

Pontius Pilate thought Jesus was innocent and asked the crowd,
"This man has done nothing wrong. What would you have me do with him?" "Crucify him!" the crowd yelled back.

Under Roman law, Pontius Pilate had the power to set one prisoner free during Passover.

"Whom shall I set free?" he asked the crowd. "This man Jesus or this common murderer, Barabbas?"

"Set Barabbas free," they shouted. "Crucify Jesus!"

"Very well," he said. "You shall have your way. Barabbas will be set free, but Jesus will be crucified!"

Carrying the Cross

MATTHEW 27, MARK 15, LUKE 23, JOHN 18-19

Jesus was handed over to some Roman soldiers who beat and whipped him until he was very weak. As he lay on the ground bleeding, the soldiers began to laugh at him and mock him.

"Oh, Your Majesty," said one of them. "I've made a special crown for you."

And he put a crown made of thorns on Jesus's head.

"Here's your royal robe," jeered another soldier, putting an old purple shawl around Jesus's shoulders.

Then it was time for Jesus to carry the cross, on which he would be nailed, to the place of crucifixions. He stumbled through the streets bearing the heavy, wooden cross on his back. Behind him, the Roman soldiers were taunting him and whipping him on.

After a while, Jesus did not have the strength to stand. So the soldiers told a man they saw in the crowd to help Jesus carry the cross. This man's name was Simon.

"Only Jesus could have done this," said one of the disciples.
Peter was so excited to see Jesus again he swam to the shore to greet him. By the time the others caught up, Jesus had already lit a fire.
"Let us cook some of the fish you caught," he said.
After eating, Jesus asked Peter if he loved him.
"You know I do," replied Peter.
Jesus asked him the question twice more. Each time Peter gave the same reply, "You know I do."
Jesus smiled and, hugging Peter, told him he should always care for the other disciples.

The Last Word

ACTS 1

The last time the disciples saw Jesus was on the Mount of Olives. He had come to say goodbye to them.

"You must speak bravely and honestly about me," said Jesus. "You must spread God's teachings to the furthest parts of this country, and to people from other countries, too. In this way the Word of God and His love will spread throughout the whole world."

Then a mist came down and covered Jesus so that the disciples could not see him anymore. When the mist cleared, Jesus had disappeared. He had been taken to Heaven to be with his Father, Almighty God, and to sit by His side forever.